If You Hadn't Survived

Alex Hedges

Alex Hedges

ISBN: 979-8-9943770-0-0

Author's Note -

If You Hadn't Survived is a collection of my original poems. They all cover heavy topics.

Publishing this collection means the world to me, and there will be more to come. I've always dreamt of being an author, so I'd like to thank everyone who has believed in me throughout this entire process, especially my friends, family, and everyone I've met along the way.

Thank you for helping me reach for my dreams; none of this would have been possible if I hadn't survived.

Alex Hedges

Trigger Warning

If you are sensitive to themes of suicide, depression,
eating disorders, grief, self-harm, or chronic illness,
please skip specific sections or don't read this book
at all.

Take care of yourself.

The Lows

Forgive Me

Forgive me for the words I have sewn together here,
I know they reek of woe
But my poetry depicts all that I cannot show,
And as I depart, I hope that I go without it,
That as I decay, my words will thrive and grow

Paint me poisoned by the idea of death,
Plagued by the pull of a final breath
I write this poem in a sort of trance,
Knowing that there is no second chance
Deep down, I know that for death I am well-suited
My begging for help has long been muted

I fail here, I stall
I surrender here, to death's call

It is all I hear, and the tugging torture is all I feel
Deep down, I know that I'll never heal

I have accepted that my writing will never satisfy
I have accepted that I am soon to die

Forgive me for leaving,
I know that I will only be immortal and breathing
through the suffering of the grieving
This ache will never fade, and I know that they're
all better without, I have no doubt
That their lives will improve, that far from this they
will move

Forgive me for the words I have sewn together here,
I know they will never agree
But I have lost all that is me
I have been drowning for so long
And now, all I hear is death's gentle song

My stories stall, and my frame surrenders to fate
Deep down, I know that I am beyond saving, that it
is too late

I cannot pretend that I have not fabricated my end
with care
I cannot pretend that I beg not to exist anywhere

I'm going nowhere
For safety, I cannot swear

Please, I plead, forgive me
All I've ever wanted is to be free

And I have cherished my words, I have cradled my
writing
Stories and poetry have allowed me to put future in
new lighting

But all is dark now
And so, I must take my final bow

Forgive me for the words I have sewn together here,
I know they reek of woe
But I have been rotting, so, so slow

Alex Hedges

Silent sweeps the night as I write my last goodbye
I've known for a long time that I was soon to die

You are Fading, Do You Notice?

Do you notice that you are fading?
The signs are erupting from the ground, shooting
into your gaze with booming sound
You walk right past them as if you don't notice, as if
death is your only focus

Do you recognize that you are fading?
Do you think as you lie still on the floor, or is it a
concern you will continue to ignore?
Unable to stand up from where you decay, this is
something you cannot downplay
Will you attempt to rise once night falls and the air
bites brisk, or will you shrug off that you are at
risk?

Do you see that you are fading?
The pale complexion devoid of hope, does it not
worry you that you cannot adequately cope?
The hollow cheeks and soulless eyes, are you aware
that in your mind, death is the only prize?
Scraggly knotted hair, staring at life with an empty
glare, does it not engulf you in flooding despair?

Do you hear that you are fading?
Do the sobs resound from a land in the distance, or
do you simply not recognize your pleading for the
end of your existence?

Alex Hedges

Can you recognize your voice, mumbling to
yourself that you have no other choice?
Are you too disconnected from reality to understand
the feeling you must flee?

Do you feel that you are fading?
The ridges on your skin, the symbolism of what's
within
Do your hands glide over your body with trembling
anguish?
Do you realize how desperately you wish to vanish?
Do they terrify you, the lines scattered about your
arms?
Doesn't death set off any internal alarms?

You are fading,
Do you notice?

Can you recognize the signs?
Can you see that what is suffocating you is
depression with its relentless vines?
Can you hear their creak and groan, can you feel
them tightening around your limp body until no part
of you is shown?
You are fading, do you notice?

Do you understand that you can no longer recognize
the stranger in your reflection?
Do you comprehend that in life, you have no more
affection?
Does it appeal to you, the way that your face has
been smeared sourly blue?
Does your chest ache as your heart thumps, unsure
of for whom it beats and pumps?

You are fading,
Do you notice?

You are fading, it is true.
Whether you fill with life again (or not) depends on
you.

I Have

I hope you know that I have long suffered

My skin sits as a sacrifice to my slicing sorrow,
laden with the blood of what I despise
I belong to hatred, with his sharp gaze and jarring
eyes

My starved stomach shrinks and shrivels, poisoned
by the burden of rivalry
I am my worst opposer; I plague my own privacy by
writing about recovery

My lungs carry all that I cannot hold
As I choke, cut off from air, stolen from words, I
will turn cold
I become all that I loathe, all that I detest
I behave as if by death I am blessed

I hope you know that I have long suffered

My eyes dim and my mouth turns, I cannot stand
myself, and I seek my own annihilation
I surrender here, for I have soured, and I am my
own worst creation

Death, I know well; him, I have not newly
discovered
And so, I hope you know that I have long suffered

I Woke Up Dead This Morning

Watched myself from above
Sick discomfort swelling within
Drained of life and love
Pale blue skin

Foam lathering my chin
Eyes wide and glossed over
I wonder what I could've been
I'll never get closure

I woke up dead this morning
In still air, an unmoving world
No warning
Before I simply became a corpse twisted and curled

Stiff carcass behind the door
Alone
Colorless hands outstretched, extending to the floor
I should've known

I woke up dead this morning
Away from my body, I drifted
It makes sense, I'll think, my world was burning
But maybe the flames could've lifted

I'll face my frame
My heart will soften
I am to blame
But it happened so quickly, so sudden

I'm not sure I deserved to die
I'm only seventeen
But death, I couldn't defy
Didn't even have the chance to get clean

I woke up dead this morning
My heart aches as I watch myself

I woke up dead this morning
Thought it would bring me comfort, my end
But I only feel the kind of despair, hurt, and agony
you can never mend

I woke up dead this morning
I thought it would be for the better, but that idea is
beginning to sever
Thought it would all be fine, thought it would be
divine

But I stand here now, staring at my carcass

Choking, in regret, I am soaking
Unable to move

I woke up dead this morning
But I had so much more to prove

After You Killed Yourself

The morning after you killed yourself,
Your body lay alone for hours after you gurgled
through your last breath with a groan
Your gruesome death went unseen, so you lay
lifeless on your bedroom floor, the corpse of a
once-vibrant teen
You killed yourself, you did it, before to anyone,
your agony, you got to admit

The morning after you killed yourself,
Your sibling swung open your bedroom door to
glance with horror at your body, lifeless on the floor
Silence swept before bellowed their cries, begging
you desperately to open your eyes
Your pet joined them beside your body, blue,
placing its head on your still stomach and curiously
awaiting play, preparing for your cue

The morning after you killed yourself,
Your parents stumbled, blindsided, into your space,
for you left with no trace
Clutching your lifeless body and shaking you in
woe, screeching your name and watching grief
tower above them as time began to slow
The pain of loss crashed through their limbs as they
wailed and wept, attempting to desperately imagine

a reality in which, as you took your life, they hadn't
peacefully slept

The morning after you killed yourself,
An emergency dispatcher listened in terror as your
sibling set the scene, describing to them the person
you had been
Sending soundless sirens and vehicles in no rush to
save, your future faltered, and you only exist now
on an ashen grave
They'd remember the way your body fell loose, and
the devastation of your family, they'd attempt to
diffuse

The morning after you killed yourself,
The coroner gazed at your chart with eyes wide;
another victim of an invisible illness had died
They'd wonder if anyone had seen your sunken
eyes or the torment in your guise
They'd write their report in need of support,
thinking of their own child, if they had been
deceived when they smiled

The afternoon after you killed yourself,
Notifications pinged, and home phones rang as the
announcement was made, words exchanged of how
they'd all wished you'd have stayed

Your mother gently closed your bedroom blinds,
sitting aside your father, the two wondering if you
had thought yourself a bother
Envisioning you sitting before them, full of lively
light, carrying no burdens you'd face secretly and
alone at night

The afternoon after you killed yourself,
Your sibling crumpled solitaire into your favorite
living-room chair, cradling themselves in their own
cold hands with a clutch so tight they could break,
giving in to their harrowing heartbreak
Your pet sat perched aside your closed bedroom
door, clawing and tapping at it lightly and making
sound only slightly, listening confusedly to your
parents sobbing, a routine which would become
nightly

The night after you killed yourself,
People congregated in the cold, holding lovely
flowers and flinching as they exchanged knowing
and painful words that you'd never grow old
They'd look to the ground and wish they could've
seen the warnings before, in your mind, you
drowned
All who knew you would unleash their version of
blame, bringing themselves to shame and wailing,
while in your name, everyone lit a flame

The night after you killed yourself,
Calmness failed to glide and sweep over all that you
knew; nobody would understand exactly what you
had to go through
Behind your death, there would lie a wake of
despair, for after hearing your name, there would
always be a stillness in the air
People unsure of how to describe the tragedy of a
life unlived and undone, wondering whether they
could've recognized the sorrow in your eyes the day
your plan had begun

The week after you killed yourself,
Your parents withered in the loss of a child,
decaying as your cherished items, they dreadfully
compiled

The month after you killed yourself,
Your house stood lifeless and still, as if you had
sucked the air from it with a terrifying will

The year after you killed yourself,
You remained unforgotten; anyone who had ever
known you would remember the way you so
fatefully perished under thoughts rotten

After you killed yourself,
Your memory lives on, but you, the glory and the
cherished, are gone.

Alex Hedges

In Case You Decide To Stay

Bundles of flowers, mourning-dove white
A dull chapel with dim, stale light
A closed casket carried by the despairing
Death is never sparing

Clenched hands caressing the filed wood
Glossy eyes fixed on where the lost should've stood
Printed pictures passed around, wails echoing with
guttural sound
Shouting as you're lowered into the ground

Know it, recognize
I'm writing about your demise

Shoulders crushed beneath the burden of woe, as
piled dirt drowns you down below
You're enclosed, encased, and erased from the
world
They're screaming your name
Begging for someone to answer, how you
surrendered so willingly to your own twisted game

Know it, recognize
I'm writing about your demise

The way you're going, an early grave calls
You will be what falls
You will surrender, you will go
Down to where the roots and roses grow

Know it, recognize
I'm writing about your demise

Lights flickering in the early dawn, matches lit to
honor the dead and gone
Balloons released into the open, if only you had
spoken
Biting lips upon mention of your name, first they'll
remember your mauled figure, your twisted frame

They'll never be the same
Daunting, dreadful dreams about what you became
Know it, recognize
I'm writing about your demise

Before it happened, nobody knew
That they'd lose such a person, someone like you
Gaping holes in hearts, and people torn apart
The consequences of a loss so grand, a kind of grief
nobody can stand

Know it, recognize
I'm writing about your demise

The way you're going, an early grave calls
You will be what falls
You will fade away in a slow and agonizing way
I'm writing this just in case you decide to stay

The Loss

Without You

Raw, reddened eyes burdened with grief, dragging
on and barely hanging on to any hopeful belief
Space aside my fragile trembling frame, an absence
that promises I'll never feel the same
Flailing helplessly in a life I never thought I'd go
through: a life without you.

From nearly untouched sheets, I will rise feebly,
looking around weakly
For your presence I yearn, and so as I avoid your
urn and gaze outside, my entire body will burn
The kind of pain you can't wish away, the kind that,
as you thrash and howl, it will simply prowl and
stay

Gazing out and a hollow presence from above, grief
is purely another form of love
In reality, we are both lifeless, only you decay as I
crumble under the weight of losing someone so
priceless
In gentle wind, trees will sway, and birds will
twitter, and beneath a blanket of woe, I will shrivel
into something bitter

I will collapse into a sea of dust, wondering if ever
again I will feel with anyone else that same level of
trust

The kind of love that swallows and the kind of grief
that follows swiftly, the type of mourning that
makes you wonder if in a year there are five
thousand weeks or only fifty
In my soul, you will never be seen as replaceable,
and putrid disgust eats at me when I question if you
ever thought of yourself as erasable

Without you,
I live in an absent state, simply anticipating my final
date
And I will never come to
Until the day my body fades cold and blue, and at
last I can finally see you

But I exist now - alive, experiencing a new kind of
living that you would disallow
I'll suffer as maggots of anguish suck the joy from
every inch of my being, knowing deep down that
with my way of living, you'd be disagreeing

The empty glass bottles, the cut-up 'inspo' board
made of magazine models
The rotting food in the sink, the unwillingness to
speak or think

The stained tissues stuffed into the bin, the one song
on repeat that'll just continuously spin
The consequences of loving someone and knowing
that death will always win

You'd wince at my guttural wails, you'd frantically
wave a white flag at my red sails
You'd know that without you, despair prevails

Breathing slowly now, through every worthy aspect
of life, my mourning has seemed to plow
We both know I can't live without you, but we
cannot rewrite the past anew
And so, in silence I stand, weary and shaking with a
kind of despair that urges me to surrender to its
demand

"Give me a sign," I'll mutter, chapped and bloody
lips trembling as my sobs splutter
Everything will remain the same, and I'll question if
this is all a sick game where the world watches as I
perish in flame

And soon, like a pounding drum, an idea will come
The thought that when you love someone - the way
I adore you - you can do anything for them, the way
I live for you.

Soulless Home

The house is empty, without you
Of our family, you were the glue, for this house,
you held a love so true

This house is soulless without you

Your paintings have been taken down, in the white
wall space, we could all drown
They're absorbing the silence, barren and plain, and
I'm going insane
Spaces once filled with beauty are now blank, for
the life in this house we had you to thank

The antique furniture has been dragged away,
watching all of it go would've painted your face
gray
Gone are the pieces you savored; this end was never
favored
No more is there glory found in every drawer, no
more is there giddiness in opening every ancient
door

The grandfather clock no longer clicks in song with
every second, which I never could've reckoned
Your mugs and glasses have been sold or kept, this
emptiness reminds me of the way I wept

If You Hadn't Survived

Family dividing your belongings with care, your
death was so unfair

Your gleeful steps no longer resonate on the floor,
and you no longer throw your hands up, greeting
people at the door
Your laugh cannot be heard anymore, though I will
still listen for it in this hollow silence until it sickens
me in my core
From this feeling, I'll try to depart, but I'll find that
I'm unable to start, I'm souring under the breaking
of my heart

This house is soulless without you

You were the light, and now I struggle to write
The embodiment of a home, your smile led to the
safety of all those who were out to roam
The loss of our lives, I'll bawl as grief stabs at me
like a thousand knives

A life once lived, now seen from above, you
illuminated this house with love
And now, within it, I stand silent, holding back
mournful wails, violent
Gazing at the white walls in this empty house with
such a cold bite, it's so dim here without your light

This house is soulless without you

Alex Hedges

She Was The Sun

The last day I saw the sun,
I hardly recognized the shell she had become

Once,
I'd known her hands to be soft as silk, radiant and
flushed
Before sickness crushed

Once,
I'd known her laugh to echo, her brilliance to
emanate with a joyful hue
Before death took his cue

The last day I saw the sun,
She gurgled and groaned with the ache of living in
agony, in pain
I knew then that I'd never be the same

Her goodbyes weren't sweet; they were brutal and
piercing, the kind that made my insides twist
She knew then that she'd be missed

The last day I saw the sun,
Our eyes met, and I wept, crumbling beneath the
weight of loss
From her, I sat across

Trembling legs, burning cheeks, mouth agape
Wailing as they gingerly pulled over the drape

She was the sun
She was *someone*

She carried with her a glow that shimmered and
shone
A smile that assured me I was never truly alone

Sweet memories and lines of time sewn together
into a braid
A light I thought would never fade

But the darkness came quick
I'd never experienced such deep, desolate despair
until she got sick

When her ever-shining light began to dwindle and
flicker
And reality tore through my throat like searing
liquor

She was the sun
She was *someone*

Gone now, away somewhere
Drowning in despair

The loss of someone, the loss of the sun
The darkness won

And so, now, I waste away
In despair, crumbling, legs beginning to sway
I wish every day
For a reality where she'd stay

Where the light never dissolved
Where death never got involved

Where she was never stolen, never gone
Where death didn't sing his eerie song

Alas, here I lie, with no light, no one
Crumbling and cracking with the loss of *someone*

She was the sun.

Untitled, for there are no words

The day before you died, we lay together on your
bed and gazed out of the window for hours
Your eyes darted about the scenery as you tried to
soak it all up, for you recognized this day would be
your last
I knew it too, and I watched your lips purse with
acceptance, and your fingers curl around your
blanket, clutching it tightly as they shook faintly

The day before you died, I recorded your voice
You spoke of Chicago summers and peaches so ripe
you'd laugh as each bite would send more dripping
down your arms, sitting beside your father with a
toothy grin
The sun would kiss you both gently, and you
warmed slowly under its blanket of glistening heat

The day before you died, you assured me you'd be
proud of me no matter what my future held
I bit my lip and fought back tears, staring at the
shimmering glass before us
Neither of us looked at the other

The day before you died, I told you how much I
loved you
I think you would have hugged me

Instead, I held your hand stiffly, as if I could keep
you with me

The day before you died, the house was noiseless
The ticking of your favorite grandfather clock
resonated in the living room, and I sat in silence on
the couch
I did not dare turn to look at your closed bedroom
door, for I knew what was coming

The day before you died, we ate your favorite
dinner for your last meal
You ate quietly with our help and spoke with a
smile of nostalgia when you reminisced about the
meal of your childhood
I tried to smile for you as you tried to smile for me

The day before you died, I grieved as you slept with
your stuffed bear
Your world was ending whilst mine slowly broke
I sobbed shiny tears of despair, and covered my
mouth, careful to be unheard

The day you died,
I lay by your side once again
This time, we barely spoke

If You Hadn't Survived

The day you died,
I choked on my words, and my tears stifled all that I
wished to say

The day you died,
You smiled at me weakly, told me you'd be okay
You said it to convince both of us,
I'm not sure we believed it

The day you died,
I crumpled to the floor in agonizing grief
I cried out your name, but there was no answer
What a cruel thing, cancer

The day you died,
A part of me died, too.

And now that it's your birthday,
I can only think of you.
My Beppe.

The Emptiness

ED

Shielded scales and biting nails
Shrieking sounds and hospital gowns
Shimmering eyes and desperate cries

A glance at the food and a shift in mood
A sinking feeling and a hospital ceiling
A nurse's gaze, polite, and the expectation of a bite

Vases of plastic flowers, blocks, and towers
Vacant couches and circles of patients with defeated
slouches
"Vacation leave" and families preparing to grieve

Empty faces and cold gazes
Eager dieticians and those with withering conditions
Early morning vitals and new patient arrivals

Machines to feed the decaying and sick minds
playing
Movement forbidden and calories hidden
Mindful therapy meant to calm and sobbing, "I
can't go on"

Alex Hedges

Emotional evenings and positive posters without
meaning
Eyes droopy and minds loopy
Endless anguish and hopeless language

S
S
S

A
A
A

V
V
V

E
E
E

M
M
M

E
E
E

Alex Hedges

S
A
V
E

M
E

Please
Save me
From my own tortured mind and body combined

The Scale

You hold the scale as if it'll save,
You cradle it with maternal care, its love is all you
crave

You cherish it gingerly,
Like it's not the source of your every injury

As if the glass doesn't tear through your flesh,
Breaking skin, searing through muscle, raw and
fresh

You cherish it as if its numbers aren't all you hear,
As if it has any empathy for your fear

You cherish it as if it were human, wrapping gentle
arms around,
You behave as if to it you are bound

You hold the scale as if it'll save,
A leaden life vest that'll drag you to an early grave

In thrashing waters you'll search for its glowing
light, for numbers of perfection,
Until for yourself you harbor no affection

You'll chase it until the mirror only holds a being
cruel, careless, and cold,
Until its control takes hold

You fade in fear of getting weighed,
And you hold the scale as if it'll save

But these roaring waters will slam down with one
final wave,
And as you drown, you'll recognize something I
think you always knew

The scale is killing you

I was Never Going to Win

Far too young to comprehend the battle set to begin,
far too young to grasp that I was never going to win
A mind tainted by its own perception, when did I
see the figure in the mirror as a being based on
misconception?
How long did it take me to realize that I was never
going to win?
How deceived was I by the false glory of being
fatally thin?

I was never going to win

Ten and doodling an admirable body with a dark
pen
Staring at the girl on the page, the moment that I
began placing the bars to my own cage
Bit my lips and let them bleed, yielding to the
understanding that perfection is all I need
I was never going to win

Eleven and clutching the belief that my body had
been horribly wrong since seven
Standing before the glass and picking anxiously at
my skin, gawking in vain at my face and chin
Then it began, the desire to lose myself to prove
that I'm better than

I was never going to win

Twelve and into the logistics of self-slaughter, I
began to delve
A thirst for perfection and an obsession with diet
culture, becoming my own vulture
Picking myself apart to the bone, screaming out, but
completely alone
I was never going to win

Thirteen and working myself weary as I soured,
mean
Seeking validity in collapse, basking in evidence of
relapse
Nobody would notice, nor would they see, that I
was held down in the darkness beneath chains,
weighty
I was never going to win

Fourteen and traveling through time like a decaying
machine
Faltering with no fuel, looking at what could save,
and allowing my mouth to drip with drool
In agony, allowing my insides to shrink, unable to
feel, move, or think
I was never going to win

Fifteen and suffocating in the routine
Decomposing in a regime lethal, mourning the
ability to find any of this rewarding or gleeful
Allowing the symptoms to resound like roaring
thunder, soon to be six feet under
Crumbling, weak and shaky, with skin flaky,
suffering as all was achy
I was never going to win

Sixteen and attempting to regrow the living scene
Glancing back at the debris, away from the damage,
I can no longer flee
With every second looking with longing and
trembling with the urge, hoping that away will fade
this surge
Though it will return, for control and perfection,
once again, I will yearn
I was never going to win

Seventeen and clean
Maybe not for long, maybe again the sound of
chaos will play its dreadful song
And maybe again I will drown, maybe I'll never get
up the next time I plummet down
But no matter the outcome, I may not fall numb to
the fact that with me will forever spin,
I was never going to win

I was never going to win

Alex Hedges

The Bells

Skin like granite, grey and lined
Sounds of static drowning out peaceful song
Here, despair and death have intertwined
Recovery and I don't get along

Eyes hollow like weathered shells, death is
sounding his ringing bells
And as I stray from living and hope, there is only
one way I can cope

Pale tile and obsession, thoughts compile
Locked door and sinking to the floor
Life is nothing but a meaningless trial
I am what I abhor

Scales and frail nails
Crazily counting and death shouting
His sound is all I hear, his shrieking wails
As his slender fingers tilt the bells, their sound
rattling, seeds of agony are sprouting

Ideas of hopelessness, of nothing ahead
In this bathroom, I'll hold my breath
This moment, this is what I dread
In my direction sweeps death

If You Hadn't Survived

He carries with him his bell, poisoning still air with
a putrid, rank smell
Circling around as I spiral, thoughts roaring,
recovery and relapse warring

This is a battle I stall to win
The eerie bell is all hear
I'll never be perfect, never truly thin
I can't handle living like this, living here

This sound, this warning
Death is beckoning, calling my name
If I continue on this way, I will fail to rise one
morning
Living means turning away from this twisted game

The bells, they slice through the air
They tear me apart, they gnash at my flesh, they
scrape at my bones
I exist nowhere
Completely alone

The bells, they mean the end of my existence
They fail to expect my persistence

These bells, they prey on my body, on my frame
They are to blame
For the fear, the fury, the feeling of fate
The idea that I am too far gone, that it is too late

The sound won't be all I hear forever
I know it, deep down
One day, I will look back at this endeavor
Thankful that in this noise, I didn't drown

Death calls, his bells ringing,
But hope is singing
Quietly, with caution, a small idea sets itself free
Which sound I listen to depends on me

Numbers and Scales

Constant distress, the kind that crawls and claws
beneath skin when you undress
It slithers between your every thought, noxious
slime, making sure the wrong battle is fought
A brawl for perfection, the kind of obsession with
numbers and scales that points you in a dangerous
direction

Like a parasite, it exists, the kind of self-hatred that
persists no matter the numbers written on your lists
The logs of all consumed as you're swallowed by
the all-consuming, the secrets you guard before
your family can even begin assuming
You'll protect these numbers as if they're your
secret wonders, stopping at no end to rid yourself of
imperfection and past blunders

Numbers and scales, entities so haunting that they'll
screech like chalkboard and nails
A deafening sound that muffles everything else
around, you won't even comprehend their control
until you've already drowned
And while you're wailing beneath churning seas
with arms flailing, they will somehow make you
feel like you're failing

Failing at what you've sacrificed everything for,
failing at thinness and perfection, aimless chores
Failing at maintaining all that you wanted control
over, failing at turning your shoulder
Failing at isolating and lying, failing at dying

Numbers and scales, the train that careens towards
you once you're tied to the rails
And unless you begin calmly exhaling and don't
even consider bailing, you will still be failing

You fail until you die; it won't matter to the
numbers and scales how hard you try

And so, as they demand every ounce of life from
your outstretched hands, you must remember your
childhood plans
Your ambitions and your goals, your future before
numbers and scales latched onto the controls, and in
your body, gouged gaping holes

The ideas that you cherished before you became a
victim of entities that push you to perish
In this battle, only one of you can fail, and read my
words closely: *It must be the numbers and the scale.*
In this battle, only one can make it through, and
read my words closely: *It must be you.*

If You Hadn't Survived

It must be you, because otherwise, you will never
live knowing what it's like to make it through
It must be you, because otherwise you will never
live the life you deserve, the one way overdue
It must be you, because otherwise you will never
learn to live with a mindset new

In a world that amplifies numbers and scales, it
must be you who learns to look at yourself and love
every single one of the details.
It must be you.

The Maladaptive

The Rollercoaster

Buckled in and blistering skin,
Another ride is about to begin
Bruised and bleeding,
To escape from this restraint, I've been forever
pleading
Alarms blaring, this rollercoaster is never sparing,
And away from reality, I am already tearing

Ineffective,
This rollercoaster has deemed love subjective
I raise my hands in hesitation,
The worn-down tracks are losing their foundation
Deep breath before this version succumbs to my
death, closed eyes
A new persona will arise

A rumble and a shout,
She'll go flying down this fatal route
The wheels will screech as the tracks plummet
down,
In her mind, she's beginning to drown
Through a treacherous tunnel, the carriage will go,
Now is when the journey starts to slow

Her complexion will pale and grey; to this low she's
fallen prey

As the darkness comes, she'll bow her head; this is
the part that I dread
She'll allow her limbs to fall numb, she'll daydream
of only one outcome

She'll suffocate,
Unable to keep her thoughts straight
She'll lose the features in her face,
I'm gone, vanished with no trace
She'll plan the end; it takes up all of her thought
She'll seek death as if I've never fought

She'll forget the rollercoaster on which she slumps,
her mouth will hang open lifelessly as the carriage
carries her through the bumps
Until a small light emerges, and away fade the urges
She'll sit straight, suddenly aware of a glorious fate,
Though there is more, she'll believe she's won the
war

The light will blind, and she'll writhe as it radiates
through her mind
Joyous explosions, untouchable and flying emotions
She'll scream until she cries; she'll believe she's
never before experienced such highs

At the light, she'll hurl all her money,
Beneath the shimmering, she'll find everything
funny

She'll grin and ignore the ache of euphoria's ploy,
She'll find that living is truly something she'll enjoy
Her eyes will remain unsleeping and unfocused,
Nobody has observed or noticed

A squeak and a boom, she'll feel as though her
future is beginning to bloom
She'll reach and she'll grasp for the imaginary;
she'll forget all that she carries
She'll aim to sprint for the light until she is again
reminded of the night

The rollercoaster will slow and steady,
For something determined, I am ready
She will fade,
And I will return to gaze at the damage she's made

As time begins to seep in, with her, I will try to
check in
But she has taken her bow and is gone now, I won't
see her until again through my life she wills to plow
Maybe she'll return soon, but for now, as I claw at
my seatbelt, I only hear the all-familiar tune
Buckled in and blistering skin,
Another ride is about to begin

"Just one more time"

"Just one more time,"
You'll whisper as your body slumps into the
piercing cold tile
In your mouth, a blend of blood and bile
Shaking as adrenaline courses through your veins
Pinched fingers as you prepare for the pains
It's better to live with scars rather than on the cover
of stacks of melancholy memoirs

"Just one more time,"
You mutter, but do you mean these words that you
utter
Or will you once again succumb to the alarm once
you turn away from your self-harm?

"Just one more time,"
You'll think as you glare with a hardened stare at
the piled-up plate that you sit before
Counting calories in a losing game and keeping a
precise score
You'll gravitate to food in every empty corner of
your diminishing mind
Your thirst for control is robbing you blind
It'll never feel enough
This is a battle you'll never win, no matter how
determined, how tough

"Just one more time,"
You mutter, but do you mean these words that you
utter
Or will you forever fight the cravings of an addict?
Will you really never again restrict?

"Just one more time,"
You'll assure yourself as your frame trembles with
demand
Succumbing to the pills in your hand
Curling up on your creaky bed, eyes bloodshot red
Decomposing as a withering body on the tainted
bedspread
A brain morphed to adhere to the needy screams of
fear
Your own desperate howling for a fix is all you hear

"Just one more time,"
You mutter, but do you mean these words that you
utter
Or will you stand holding a white flag, waving,
surrendering to every vicious craving and
abandoning your own saving?

"Just one more time,"
You'll promise everyone as you turn them away
Crumpling under loneliness, as to your thoughts,
you become prey

You'll ignore the alarms ringing within you,
indicating exhaust
Eyes painfully glossed
You'll watch yourself helplessly as you spiral
another time
With no will to again look up to healing and climb

"Just one more time,"
You mutter, but do you mean these words that you
utter
Or will you struggle endlessly to clamber away
from self-sabotage, will the thoughts, optimistic and
cruel, always together camouflage?

"Just one more time,"
You'll glance in the mirror, preparing yourself for
what lies ahead
Begging for it to end with you dead
Awaiting the last and final blow
Worsening to a point of no return, with horrific
ideas of perfection in tow
The itch to endorse your sinking to a grim rock
bottom, and declare yourself unsavable with no
remorse

"Just one more time,"
You mutter, but do you mean these words that you
utter

Or are you simply choking on your own coping
skills? Will you ever survive if you continue to
hopelessly look for dangerous ways of seeking
thrills?

"Just one more time,"
You'll quietly croak on your dying day, for the way
you cope does not keep death away

Alex Hedges

The Itch

My world is coming to an end
Once again, the itch will return
I'm failing to pretend
Once again, my skin will burn

The itch, it comes crawling
Seeping into my movements, into my arms
Under my skin, it'll creep as I begin falling
Quiet will sound the alarms

The itch, it convulses my hands, I'll watch them
twitch
The desire to breathe
Drowning in apathy, in my hopelessness, I lay rich
And so I'll pull up my sleeve

The itch, it shakes my soul
Unable to think, unable to focus
Unsheathing the object that I stole
Tears will stream, and nobody will notice

The itch, it surges alone
Scrambling my insides
A canvas that must be sewn
Watching in horror as artwork divides

The itch, it suffocates
All I feel
With my hands threatening potential fates
I'll never stop, I'll never heal

The itch, it's back
I'm shriveling
I can't keep track
Of time while death is whistling

My world is coming to an end
Once again, the itch will return
I'm failing to pretend
Once again, my skin will burn

My life is coming to a close
The itch comes crashing
Time and time again, soaking my stained clothes
Under its violence, I will surrender, stop my
thrashing

The itch, it's back
But now, it's all going black
Maybe from this I'll learn - or maybe it's my turn
I've never before felt this kind of burn

The itch, it's gone
I lie lifeless as early comes the dawn
The itch and I, we couldn't live on

Alex Hedges

The itch, it's gone

Hunted

You paint yourself pained prey, with eyes touched
by innocence, fragile and weak
You walk gingerly, and you do not dare speak

You deem yourself the hunted, the kind of being
one betrays
I'll tell you this now: you will die this way

You paint yourself pained prey, kissed by doom
But soon, the crown of a killer, you will assume

For you starve what you believe to be vile
You loathe life, and you despise your thighs, your
arms, your smile

You cradle pearly dots in your palms, addicted to
what calms
And you choke as you suffocate solace in sweet
smoke
You skin your knees on bathroom tile and gag on
your own misery just to please

You trip on train tracks and wait, backing away
right before
You endanger what you abhor

You paint yourself pained prey, but know this as
you drag yourself down under,

You are your own hunter

The Angst

The Glass

She who sees life ahead lies with frosted eyes that
invite no light
And so, the shattered glass of future decorates the
floor on this dull night

You bury her here, a skeleton of hope
You know what it is to punish, I see it in the way
you cope

You yank yourself through agonizing flames, you
drag metal along
You mutilate yourself, you aim to slaughter what is
wrong

Your teeth catch on your knuckles, and your
bloodshot eyes shine with shame
You know suffering, and you know pain

You stand now atop fragments of future, slicing and
soaked in blood, sour
And you paint yourself a person without power

Though I hope you allow yourself to recover loudly
There was once a time when you cradled this glass,
you held it tight

And you once knew what it was to fight
I know you surrendered your glow, I know you beg
to go

Alex Hedges

I stop you here only for a second, split
I know you plead for it

But you and fate cannot yet mix
For you have broken glass to fix

Bugs

Bugs crawling beneath skin, a metaphor for what's
within
Wrists and thighs are buzzing like flies, critters
clawing at what I despise
My body twisting and turning, their burn returning
in times concerning
Bugs slithering on my forearm, the feeling of
seeking harm

An itching beneath the skin is, in reality, a distress
in the brain, monsters whispering and bugs chirping
to justify physical pain
And so, my mind is caving, collapsing on itself to
reveal the bugs that line the paving
Each intricacy of my mind and soul is controlled by
bugs with only one goal

To harm, to collide their wings in alarm
To clamber atop every muscle, to make sure with
every crumpling thought the urge comes to sound
and rustle
To circle every bone, to encapsulate me like damp
moss to stone

Bugs buzzing and creeping, tears soaking and
seeping
Bugs clambering and crawling, a feeling of falling
Bugs gnawing and tearing, deafening urges blaring

The desire to feed the itch, to cut and sew and tie
the stitch
For the buzz to soften, it doesn't happen often
To give in, to let the bugs win - to give up and
torture my skin

If the bugs are all I ever hear, will my mind ever
truly be clear?

Without the itching limbs and the clawing of my
need, could it have been that I would never know
what it's like to really bleed?
Bugs crawling beneath skin, a metaphor for what's
within

The bugs tug at my veins, move me about like a
puppet in chains
Yank me to the bathroom floor, throw my blistered
hands up to slam the door
Twist the lock and hide the key, I'll never leave this
place, and I'll never be free

To live a prisoner to bugs, of whom I am the only
listener, living a life suffocating in gauze, when I
am the only cause
Is it a life at all, or do I only have purpose when the
bugs are falling out red in the bathroom stall?

The bugs that drown me out, do I not cradle any
doubt that they direct me on the right route?
The bugs that screech when the waves come
crashing, must I always succumb to their clawing
and gnashing?
Do I live only to wince in the darkness, to bow my
head at the bugs and their piercing sharpness?

Bugs crawling beneath skin, a metaphor for what's
within
But do they live within my every atom and cover
me whole, or over them do I still hold some
control?

Bugs crawling beneath skin, marks of how I've
been and when they've stood a chance to win
But do I really hear their wings rubbing with
dangerous flirtation, or are they really just figments
of my imagination?

I need not say that the bugs control my everyday,
but whether I continue to decay or keep the
thoughts at bay is up to me,

So is there really beneath my skin even a single flea, or does it just terrify me that I am the one who will bring me to safety?

Quality of Life

Sunken hospital beds
A body laced with wires and threads

Blaring beeping machines
Concealing your life behind the scenes

Rigid pain holding shackle and chain to your brain
The kind of ache that twists your insides while you
curl and scream in vain

The type of illness that seeps through your house
with uneasy stillness
An entity that so blatantly restricts your liberty and
holds you in woesome captivity

The type of illness that will crawl under your skin
as your mind spins in strife
The type of illness that demands the surrender of
your quality of life

And so, as it stands,
You will watch helplessly as your world slowly
disappears from your hands

Cold packs and monthly injections
Forgotten texts and butchered connections

Alex Hedges

A body of glass
The ghost of your presence fading from every
bustling crowd and class

A cycle of exhaustion and defeat
Tracing circles onto scratchy hospital blankets,
unable to greet others or even hobble down the
street

Forgotten and decaying
Staring at 'get better soon!' with hopelessness
weighing

Misunderstood and unable to move
Wasting away while everyone expects you to
improve

You'll find yourself gaping at the stranger in the
mirror
Her anguish has never been clearer

And you'll crumple as your eyes meet hers in the
reflection
Baffled by her lifeless eyes and sickly complexion

Buckets at bedsides
Symptoms that crash and fade like ruthless tides

If You Hadn't Survived

An ocean of uncertainty
The ebbing and flowing of anxious urgency

A demanding game that nobody signed up to play
Now, for its detriment, you must unfairly pay

Stuffing dreams away with dismay
Stacks of boxes filled with ambition you once held
before your health gave way

Debilitating livelihood
A feigned "I'm good" and the inability to achieve
what you once thought you would

This is your reality
This is my reality
This is the reality

And so, here I stand
Slowly succumbing to chronic illness and its
disastrous demand

Wondering with fluttering eyelids and a tear-stained
face
If I will ever heal with grace and make it out of this
place

Alex Hedges

And so, as it stands,
I will watch helplessly as my world slowly
disappears from my hands

Quality of life and chronic illness exist exclusively,
for only one of them is a villainous reality that acts
abusively,

And the other lies far out of reach
As if in my future, it only exists as a blissful figure
of speech

This is the reality of becoming the debris of an
illness that overwhelms to such a severe degree

From The Stands

I exist only to silently observe,
Plagued by illness I did nothing to deserve

Slumped atop rusted seats as I slowly decay,
Watching the lives of others as if a life alike lies
locked away

Not a single person from down below understands,
And so, I'll simply watch from the stands

I sit agitated by their indifference to the ill-fated,
Their reluctance to acknowledge those who have
long waited

I fall through time as days pass me by,
Unable to stand and unwilling to even try

Drowning in hospital gowns and darkness
all-consuming,
Sickened by the reminiscent sound of machines
blaring and booming

As my health has painted me invisible,
All of my friendships have fallen easily divisible

Alex Hedges

All I can do is sit back and attempt to distract
myself from this fact,
Attempt to ignore that the fragile walls of my heart
have cracked

Uncontrollable and out of my hands,
My illnesses paint me helpless as life goes on
outside of these dreary stands

And so, I can only allow my anger to bubble and
brew,
As my face loses all color and my lips go blue

Tears falling,
Burdened by the understanding that nobody outside
the stands will hear or recognize my bawling

Alone, I suffer while my illnesses seek to smother
in a time so dreadful that it compares to no other

There is nothing more to be said,
Everything I once dreaded has occurred, and my
vision blurs when I make any effort to think about
what lies ahead

All of the appointments, blood tests, and scans,
I have no future plans

Completely isolated from those who once knew my
every thought,
Those who now have no idea how hard for health
I've fought

And so, here I sit,
Decaying and more alone than I'd like to admit

With a crumpling body and shaking hands
A single figure watching all of you from the stands

Do you see me, at least a little bit?

Must I fall to my knees and beg and plead for some
support,
Or will you all turn your backs as my world
continues to distort?

Am I simply plagued to be forever alone in the
stands?
Must I live the harrowing life that my illness
demands, solo as all of you grow while I continue to
shatter with every blow?
Is this simply the reality of chronic illness, that my
world will slowly continue to shrink until I'm
drowning in silent stillness?

I exist only to silently observe,
Plagued by illness I did nothing to deserve

Alex Hedges

With a crumpling body and shaking hands
A single figure watching all of you from the stands

It Is Now Mine

Gowns of glistening galaxies draped over
Wires braided like intertwined vines long
Begging with each shooting star, each clover
Picturing blaring beeping as sweet song

Gaunt and rid of life, vigor fading away
Hollow cheeks and hair decorating tile
The weight of hopelessness crushing, skin gray
Forgotten frame, never the same, feigned smile

Death came sweeping in the springtime sun bright
Caressing my face and promising fate
Days dragging, eyes sagging; living took might
Whispering goodbyes, knowing it's too late

In this time, I learned what it means to shine
To hold future and say, "this is now mine"

The Hope

A Message For the Women

A message for the women

For the women
Whose voices were muffled under the deafening
boom of oppression in every room
Whose actions were shot down and covered up as
they struggled through a life so violently screwed
up
Whose silenced opinions strayed from the others,
though were left dismissed under the impression
that they'd solely amount to quiet mothers

For the women
Who walk through desolate city streets below a
shadowed moon and must stride with resilience to
deafen the gruff and violent tune
Who stay straight-faced as their insides contort,
who know to scream if the weapons they conceal
fall short
Who in hazy alleyways must call those they know,
must laugh and giggle and put on a show

For the women
Who have felt the disgust of unwarranted touch and
couldn't trust the courts as a crutch
Who were blamed and shamed for the way in which
they were horrifically maimed
Who froze or fought, whose worst nightmares
reside within cells or remain uncaught

For the women
Who have faced no opportunities to get out of the
lives that history has placed
Who have neglected what may lie within, so as not
to irritate the man whose patience runs thin
Who have spent their days hidden and who, from a
plentiful life, have been forbidden

For the women
Who have brawled for rights, who have gathered in
the nights under hope and its bright lights
Who have strangled the tedious expectations that lie
on repressive foundations
Who have become everything they've craved and
more, who have gone to war, swore, seen their goals
as a doable chore, and allowed the opposition to
succumb to their glorious roar

For the women
For the poets, for the writers, for the firefighters
For the engineers, for the farmers wielding shears
For the doctors, for the excellent proctors
For the athletes, for the musicians and their
beautiful beats
For the software developers, for the senators
For the pharmacists, for the psychologists
For the housewife, for the preservers of wildlife

For every woman so heroically strong, for every
woman who has proven a stereotype wrong
For every woman who has inspired a girl, for every
woman who, through a tedious life, is still able to
twirl

For every woman
Who feels as though their voice may not reach, or
whose doubts cling to them like a blood-sucking
leech
Who feels as though their mind is not wonderful or
who only believes she has been dwindled to just an
object fertile
Who feels as though in this world she is unsafe and
unprotected, who has never experienced what it's
like to be truly respected

Alex Hedges

A message for the women

Your voice reigns, we all hear your echoing pains
and see the way in which you lie beneath bulky
chains
Your thoughts matter, whether they flatter or
shatter; you must draw them into your chatter
You are valuable, and those who disbelieve are
laughable; you are not damnable

For the women
Who feel as though they'll never survive in a world
against them, who have fallen numb

A message for the women

You are not the scared girl that you clutch within
you,
Away from your soul, she grew

You are not the fragile one who, once, away from
evil, you had to run,
In your battle with her, you have won

You are not helpless anymore,
That version of you, you are free to abhor

A message for the women

If You Hadn't Survived

You stand now unafraid as you are; you are your
own creation, and you are the brightest star
Hold each other's hands as you stand united in the
badlands
Shake your fists at the world, for as long as hate
exists, for you can be the soul that valiantly persists

Alex Hedges

Full of Life

Fused to a scale as you drown in your demise
Paper gown and shut eyes, knowing the number
must rise
Grinning nurses and scribbled-over nutrition labels
Crumpling helplessly as recovery turns the tables

Gaunt and lifeless complexion changing in the
reflection
Bags and pockets suddenly under inspection,
And a new idea that there's beauty in imperfection

Hearing "you look so full of life!" on repeat, it's all
so bittersweet

Your eyebags will slowly fade
Eventually, it won't feel life-threatening to get
weighed
Your hair will grow back thick
Your loved ones won't feel like they're talking to a
wall of brick
Your bones will strengthen
Your list of reasons to recover will, with time,
lengthen

Hearing "you look so full of life!" on repeat, it's all
so bittersweet

At first, you won't know what life means, you've
been obsessing emptily for all of your teens

A particular type of glow will radiate from your
skin
About all of your rules, your mind will slowly stop
its spin
Your cheeks will flush with vitality
To food, you will learn a peaceful reaction of
neutrality
Your eyes will spark with passion and light
And you'll beam with every bite

Your frame will shake under the weight of the
universe
You may even crumple beneath the urge to get
worse,
But it is only recovery in which you can immerse
You must learn that life and death are not an endless
cycle you can go through and rehearse
It is not infinite, nor is it simple and blunt;
This is a lifelong roller coaster, and you will be
seated in the front

Wind whipping through your face,
Understanding that your body must take up space
Whistling and glee echoing around your ears,
Doing everything possible, no matter how badly it
whips up your worst fears

Body secure beneath the locked belt,
Knowing that you're tied to a future entangled with
a joy you've never before felt

The possibilities will tower dauntingly before you,
But even as you begin to shrink in fear, your loved
ones will comment that you seem "more you"
You're "full of life, you're glowing and free, you're
healthy now, you're happy as can be"
They will call you fuller and bigger and happier and
prettier
And although it may not be all fact, you can control
your impact

Whether or not their words ring true depends on
you,
And though new, maybe "full of life" is simply
what is supposed to be you.

The Garden

The garden was barren before; all was withered and
wilted
The wind tore through, and the whimpering, whiny
trees tilted

The garden was dead before

The dirt froze around the roots of your being,
crackling and dry
The leaves shriveled in the gale, performing what it
is to die

And you watched with wonder as all began to fade
As all decayed with death's aid

The garden was dead before

When roaring rain rampaged, burning holes in your
trembling hands
When all that grew was your poisonous plans

Spirit shrank under the burden of a final goodbye
Back when the smog of sorrow soured the sky

The garden was dead before

When you designated a day with careful detail
Before you knew what it was to try and fail

And it arrived like no other
Alongside the knowledge that there would not be
another

But when you stood on that bridge, beneath towers
of golden steel
It was warmth that you began to feel

The gentle kiss of light, swirling through what had
hardened
It was the warmth that washed over your garden

And as their hands yanked you from the rails
They formed the beginnings of new trails

While your teeth touched tattered pavement, hard
While they strapped down your skin, scarred

While sirens sang
The snaking streams hissed, and the plants sprang

Color returned, verdant, vibrant, and victorious
Life returned, glorious

The garden was dead before

If You Hadn't Survived

Though now it prospers and prevails
We see it in the swaying leaves, the singing
songbirds, the winding trails

Something you would once disallow,
The garden lives now

And it thrives with your every breath
It flourishes when you evade death

Every time the urges come crashing
And the winds are thrashing

You must remember with whom the roots lie
The one who wears your eyes

The one who screamed as you tried to go down
below
The one who, into you, will grow

I beg

The next time the wind picks up, and the dirt begins
to harden
Remember the kid who grew your garden

The one within
Every version of yourself you have ever been

Alex Hedges

The Eyes of the Past

It was earlier that I sat shaky and aghast,
Gaping at the girl opposite me and staring into the
eyes of my past
Beneath dimly lit lights, my every thought went
unsaid,
As she watched me with bitter distaste, for I wasn't
dead
She bit her lips in denial of my existence,
In shock at the sight of her eventual persistence

I watched her eyes steady,
How her body slumped as everything weighed on
her heavy
How her pupils danced about the silhouettes in the
room,
Her face twisted with the conscious understanding
of her doom
"Why are we here?" She asked
And I smiled softly as time slowly passed

"You will survive," I whispered with more care than
I'd ever held before,
I hadn't needed to say any more
She scoffed and looked away,
In the glint of her eyes, I could sense her dismay
We didn't speak or make a single sound,

I merely watched while she glared into the
background

Her inturned cheeks had each hollowed like a
darkened cave,
I knew she didn't care that she was digging her own
grave
Aware of the anguish gnawing at her arms and
thighs,
Yet all I could really look at were her eyes
The saucers of hopelessness and woe,
As it dawned on her that into me she'd grow

It haunted me slightly, the way she shifted in her
seat
My torn chest ached tightly
Stomach flipping,
Knowing what she was thinking
Recognizing the clinking in her bag, and watching
her act like nobody could tell she was sinking
Her eyes bore into the window while the voices in
her head began to take shape,
Plotting her final, fatal escape

She blinked leisurely, and I watched her eagerly
Taking note of her sagging clothes and bruised
elbows,
The ripples and rainbows of exhaustion in her face,

And the way her thoughts so obviously took up
every ounce of space
And so, with begging eyes, I looked at her,
Ignorant of the fact that her world was a blur

The moment ended when she stood suddenly
Slinking off sullenly
We shared no goodbyes or last regards,
But I knew her perspective was dissipating like I
was the wind to her house of cards
To live and look back at last
An odd experience when you look into the eyes of
your past

I rose and strode to the other side of the room,
Towards the oak door covered in flowers in full
bloom
Sighing in acceptance and understanding that those
eyes signified my demise,
Knowing that in keeping those eyes, my hope
would only die

And so, finally,
I locked my fingers around the door handle
righteously,
Turning away from the old me and pulling the door
open as I knew I should,
And as she one day would

You Will Make It

Drowning in perilous waters foaming white
As you kick and flail, you'll slowly lose hope in
your ability to fight
Steady land ceases to exist before your shaking
frame
You'll feel alone in what feels like a rigged game
You'll set the expectation and circle the date
Waiting for time to pass until you reach your tragic
fate

You'll sit in the frigid and record the voice that soon
others will mourn
Admit to your suffering, and the inability to believe
that you'll never stop feeling torn
You'll prepare your belongings and sort out
goodbyes of all types
Plan out the last moments on your calendar and its
final stripes

But before you quit, recognize the possibility that
you will make it

Though you are sputtering and choking in waves of
dismay,
Don't just yet throw everything away
The booming waters may be all you hear,

But don't just yet allow your apathy to be the
headlights to your deer
The timid animal that lives within,
The trembling child that wouldn't understand the
tears now dripping from your chin

You will make it

Roaring waters must one day fall silent
For forever, nothing can stay so violent
Your decaying body must one day begin to float
To your perpetual sinking, you must not devote
No matter how much farther you fall in these depths
unlit, you will make it

Though you may not know it now, soon this
realization will hit
You will make it

You will make it to feel the vibrations of
shimmering fireworks above
You will make it to the feeling of unfathomable love
You will make it to the cupboards of assorted mugs
you have painted
You will make it to looking at the welcoming home
you will have one day created
You will make it to confetti falling all around
You will make it to looking back in disbelief that
you could've drowned

You will make it to hugs, solemn and joyful
You will make it to surrounding yourself with those
deemed loyal
You will make it to your art exhibits
You will make it to New Year's Eve, counting down
the minutes
You will make it to moments so sweet they bring
oceans to your eyes
You will make it to the days when you no longer
live under a masked disguise

To sipping large foamy drinks by illuminated
windows
To growing old enough to call children kiddos
To laughing in the rain with outstretched hands
To appreciating the songs of the artist who
understands
To drawing figures on frosty car glass
To remember the date you once set as you drowned,
and to every year surpass

To collect reasons to live the same way you once
collected crystals hidden beneath dry dirt
To chuckle as you enjoy dessert, or throw your
hands around during a concert
To smile again
To find the ability to pick up your favorite pen

You will make it

Alex Hedges

To the life you've yearned for, to the way of living
you've earned
To what you never would've expected when your
head was underwater in the woe
To live on dry land and wince at what it was to
drown down below
You will make it, I know

You have to make it
You will make it

You have to make it to moving past the waters of
sorrow,
To growing away from the version of you that
couldn't fathom the idea of a tomorrow
To developing an ability to live on when the water
begins to pool
To see it as fuel
To grow from who you are now
To begin healing from this feeling in ways that you
once wouldn't allow

You will make it.

If You Hadn't Survived

Alex Hedges

If You Hadn't Survived, The Original

If you hadn't survived,
Life would have continued, but those who knew
you would dissolve into fragments of time and fall
into the quicksand of remembrance. With sagging
and darkened eyes, they'd gaze at old photos,
twisted by the grief they would gradually drown in.

If you hadn't survived,
Your parents would stand in your bedroom, unable
to move, staring at every organized object on your
desk, wondering if you had finally cleaned your
room for them as a last act. They would crumple
under the pain of a lost child, unable to bear the
grief clawing at their insides and tearing their skin.

If you hadn't survived,
Your sibling would sit at dinner with your parents
and look emptily at the seat next to them. They
would shake their head when your parents reminded
them to eat, and slam their door upon leaving the
table. They wouldn't be able to accept the fact that
you were gone. They would beg for one last minute
with you every night.

If you hadn't survived,
Your childhood pet would sit still in your bedroom,
waiting for your arrival. Your mother would make
desperate attempts to shoo it from where you once
sat together snuggled on the floor, but it would
whine and wait for you endlessly. It would never
accept that you won't come back.

If you hadn't survived,
Your best friends would sift through your beloved
items, holding them to their chests and allowing
grim sobs to overtake their bodies. They would sit
on the bed you once laughed on together and stare
at your favorite things, unable to accept your death.

If you hadn't survived,
Your next-door neighbor would wake in the night,
haunted by the vivid screams of your parents as
your body bag crossed the threshold to your home.
They'd walk by your house and stare at the
sidewalk, unable to walk away from the sinking
feeling in their chest.

If you hadn't survived,
Your teachers would sit at their kitchen table,
reading the email sent out. They'd rest their head in
their hands and look back at your old assignments,
staring at the drawings lining the sides, taking note
of the warning signs. It would be too late.

Alex Hedges

If you hadn't survived,
Your death would have impacted every person who
ever met you.
Heartache would've spread, and your name would
be grimly remembered

But you did.
And those people, whether you know it or not, you
impact them every day.

They look forward to seeing you.
They see you in your favorite food, your favorite
movie, your favorite show, your favorite color, your
favorite hobby, and your favorite weather.
They see you.

They love you.
You survived, and you are loved.
You survived, and you are cared for.
You survived, and you are appreciated.
You survived.

If You Hadn't Survived II

If you hadn't survived,

Those kissed by the gentle touch of familiarity
would falter, stolen from speech and robbed of
relief
In vain, they'd grasp for the absolute, flailing and
failing in the quicksand of grief

If you hadn't survived,

Your jarring name would've split still air, slicing
through
You would not be remembered for you

If you hadn't survived,

You would slowly fade away, wasting and withering
in rank, poisoned air
Honored only for what you could not bear

If you hadn't survived,

You'd exist soley in the notes you signed
In the way you and fate intertwined

Though it wasn't fate, it wasn't meant to be
I tell you this now as I tell me

If you had died, you would've missed the day hope
arrived

Alex Hedges

And if it hasn't come yet, fear not, for recovery can
be revived

So, know this now:
You would've never seen every version of yourself
you have since been if you had died
You would've never lived the moments in which
you've thrived

If you simply hadn't survived

If You Hadn't Survived

www.ingramcontent.com/pod-product-compliance
Lightning Source LLC
LaVergne TN
LVHW051423080426
835508LV00022B/3209